PENGUIN BOOKS

TIME REMEMBERED

'Miss Read', or in real life Mrs Dora Saint, is a teacher by profession who started writing after the Second World War, beginning with light essays written under her own name mainly for *Punch*. She has written on educational and country matters for various journals, and worked as a script-writer for the B.B.C.

'Miss Read' is married, with one daughter, and lives in a tiny Berkshire hamlet. She is a local magistrate and her hobbies are theatre-going, listening to music and reading.

'Miss Read' has published numerous books including *Village School* (1955), *Village Diary* (1957), *Thrush Green* (1959), *Fresh from the Country* (1960), *Winter in Thrush Green* (1961), an anthology, *Miss Clare Remembers* (1962), *Country Bunch* (1963), *Over the Gate* (1964), *The Market Square* (1966), *The Howards of Caxley* (1967), *The Fairacre Festival* (1968), *News from Thrush Green* (1970), *Tyler's Row* (1972), *The Christmas Mouse* (1973), *Farther Afield* (1974), *Battles at Thrush Green* (1975), *No Holly for Miss Quinn* (1976), *Village Affairs* (1977), *Return to Thrush Green* (1978), *The White Robin* (1979), *Village Centenary* (1980), *Gossip from Thrush Green* (1981), *Affairs at Thrush Green* (1983) and *Summer at Fairacre* (1984). She has also written two books for children, *Hobby Horse Cottage* and *Hob and the Horse-bat*, the Red Bus series for the very young, and the first volume of her autobiography, *A Fortunate Grandchild*. Many of her books are published in Penguins together with three omnibus editions: *Chronicles of Fairacre*, containing *Village School*, *Village Diary* and *Storm in the Village*; *Life at Thrush Green*, containing *Thrush Green*, *Winter in Thrush Green* and *News from Thrush Green*; and *Further Chronicles of Fairacre*, containing *Miss Clare Remembers*, *Over the Gate*, *The Fairacre Festival* and *Emily Davis*; and a collection of recipes, *Miss Read's Country Cooking*.

TIME
REMEMBERED

'Miss Read'

Illustrated by Derek Crowe

PENGUIN BOOKS

Penguin Books Ltd, Harmondsworth, Middlesex, England
Viking Penguin Inc., 40 West 23rd Street, New York, New York 10010, U.S.A.
Penguin Books Australia Ltd, Ringwood, Victoria, Australia
Penguin Books Canada Ltd, 2801 John Street, Markham, Ontario, Canada L3R 1B4
Penguin Books (N.Z.) Ltd, 182–190 Wairau Road, Auckland 10, New Zealand

First published by Michael Joseph 1986
Published in Penguin Books 1987

Made and printed in Great Britain by
Richard Clay Ltd, Bungay, Suffolk
Typeset in Bembo

To My Schoolfellows
of 1921–1924

Contents

And time remembered is grief forgotten,
And frosts are slain and flowers begotten.

From *Atalanta in Calydon*
A. C. Swinburne 1837–1909

Foreword

THIS is an unashamedly nostalgic account of one of the happiest periods of my life. It dwells on that happiness, which is why Swinburne's quotation is used here.

It was a time which shaped the pattern of my future. It brought home to me the need to live in the country, to relish the changing seasons, village diversities, and to revere those writers whose particular genius was their interpretation of English country things—Thomas Hardy, W. H. Hudson, Flora Thompson, Edward Thomas, John Betjeman, and a score more.

The impact which those three years at a Kentish village school made upon me was unusually strong—one might almost say violent—for two reasons.

First, I was at that stage of life, not quite eight years old, when one is sharply aware of one's surroundings. It is at this stage in a child's development that imagination is at its most intense, and when witches, ghosts and giants take the place of Peter Rabbit in one's reading, and when woods and secret places take on a new and thrilling intimacy. I was more than ready.

The second reason was that I had suddenly exchanged the pressure of London life for the slower ways of the country, and it suited me. I had always loathed crowds, to the point of panic, and to go shopping with my mother, pressed against counters by towering adults, was sheer misery.

Knowing only one school, from the age of four, I assumed that all schools were large, noisy and regimented, with classes of fifty or more to a room. Moreover, I imagined that pressure to strive, to push on to even more arduous efforts, was common to all schools.

As an unambitious child, I disliked this wearisome régime. I had no desire to do better than my neighbours, and lacked any envy of their abilities, looks or possessions. I soon realised that what I really wanted was time to ruminate, time to observe, and often time to be alone.

At Chelsfield I came into my own, and have never ceased to be thankful.

Brave New World

O<small>N</small> the second day of March 1921 I went with my mother to Hither Green station in South London to go to our new home.

We were bound for Chelsfield, only a few stations down the line, and I looked forward eagerly to the journey. It was a weekday, and I really should have been in school, which made the whole adventure more exciting.

I was seven years old.

In those days of the London South-Eastern and Chatham Railway the trains were steam ones, and there was something awe-inspiring about the snorting throbbing engines which made the whole station shudder when they drew in to the platform.

Smoke puffed from the chimney, and steam gushed from various points along the side of the monster. Doors clanged, porters yelled, whistles blew, flags waved—the din was tremendous. The greasy step up into the third-class carriage was almost too high for a child to mount, but we were soon ensconced on the mottled red and black seats, and able to lean back and admire the photographs of distant resorts arranged just under the luggage rack.

Should I ever see the Leys at Folkestone, and those svelte ladies walking there, with their long skirts sweeping the grass and their elaborate hats needing a gloved hand clamped on them to withstand the sea breeze? Would I ever be lucky enough to see the Toad Stone at Tunbridge Wells, or the Esplanade at Margate?

As we chuffed slowly out of the station, I could see my old school, a three-storey building of brick with stone ornamentation, identical to many others put up by the London County Council.

I had started on the ground floor there, one of many 'Mixed Infants', but fortunate in that my Aunt Rose was one of the teachers, and had taken me to school in the early days. Later, I was elevated to the second floor 'Girls' where I shared a classroom with about fifty other six and seven-year-olds and had 'real work' to do.

The boxes of beads, the wet clay balls, the sand trays and singing games were left behind. Now the day began in the classroom, after morning assembly in the hall, with ferocious attacks on multiplication tables.

Our teacher was called Miss Sanders, and that was how you addressed her. She seemed to me to be quite as old as my dear Grandma Read, but I doubt if she was more than thirty.

The blackboard was covered in columns of multiplication tables, and we began by chanting in unison.

> Four ones are four
> Four twos are eight
> Four threes are twelve
> Four fours are sixteen

and so on, until we reached the crescendo of

> Four tens are FORTY

Then the diminuendo:

> Four elevens are forty-four
> Four twelves are forty-eight.

Then we sank back. But not for long. Within seconds, Miss Sanders' red-tipped pointer would be scampering about the column while we blundered after it, faint but pursuing.

'Four sevens, four sevens, four sevens!' our teacher would yell.

'Twenty-eight!' we shouted back.

'Seven fours!' would continue our mentor fortissimo. The response would be less robust. Could seven fours be the same as four sevens? It seemed that it could.

We laboured on. Later generations would work it all out with milk bottles or Cuisenaire rods, but I doubt if any of them could match us for a completely instantaneous reaction to such challenges as 'Nine eights' in years to come.

We did an awful lot of chanting in those days, and rather liked it. Spellings, days of the week, months of the year, counting to a hundred in ones and then in twos, and sometimes in tens. We chanted a money table which began:

Four farthings one penny

and ended with the triumphant shout:

Twenty-one shillings one guinea.

And we learnt a new poem every week. (Although why seven-year-olds should be given that heart-breaking poem of Keats' beginning: 'I had a dove and the sweet dove died', I now wonder. It haunts me still.)

At playtime, in the bare asphalt wastes, there were literally hundreds of us milling about. We 'Mixed Infants' shared the space with the big girls, and watched in admiration as they skipped together chanting:

R. White's Ginger Beer
Goes off POP!

or 'Salt, Mustard, Vinegar, Pepper' followed by

counting, sometimes up to the forties or fifties, unless some duffer tripped up, amidst the groans of her fellows, and stopped the twirling rope.

There were tops, too, chalked with patterns, and whipped energetically along the asphalt with a string or leather thong on the end of a stick. Top-spinners were always in a frenzy and could be quite ferocious if one tripped over their treasure and wrecked its progress.

The noise naturally was horrendous, and it was almost a relief to hear the whistle blow and scurry into lines ready for marching indoors again.

'You will be going to Chelsfield School,' I had been told by my parents. I assumed that it would be much the same—large, noisy, busy with children, and ruled by some dozen or so teachers exhorting one to sit up, to stand straight, to stop sucking one's pencil, to work harder, to be neat, to be polite, and to be obedient. That, I took it, was what all schools were like. I felt I could face it after three years of the experience.

We chugged along steadily through Grove Park, leafy Chislehurst and Orpington. Here a vociferous porter just outside our window yelled: 'Orpington! Orpington! This train for Chelsfield! Knockholt, Dunton Green and Sevenoaks! Change at Dunton

6

Green for Chevening 'Alt, Brasted and Westerrum!'

'Chelsfield next stop,' said my mother.

I was glad to hear it. It had been a long haul, I thought, between Chislehurst and Orpington through flat fields and with not much to see. It was years later that Petts Wood came to be built on that marshy ground, and then houses covered the fields I saw on my first journey, not only there but further down the line as well.

So far, all the stations had been fairly busy, despite the fact that it was late morning and the heaviest traffic had gone. I expected stations to be busy. Until then, my railway trips had been largely up the line from Hither Green to Charing Cross, usually in the company of my maiden Aunts Rose and Jess en route to the theatre or to do some shopping.

They, with my bachelor Uncle Harry, lived at 267 Hither Green Lane with my much-loved Grandma Read. I was going to miss them all.

Even more, I was already missing the companionship of my sister Lil, then aged ten, and staying for the rest of that spring term at Hither Green Lane in order to sit a scholarship examination which would determine her future. I should see her at the weekends and when she broke up. In the summer term, no doubt, she would accompany me to the village school before moving to higher things in September.

My father had stayed behind to supervise the packing, but was to catch a later train, which accounted for this rare experience of having my mother to myself.

7

The high embankment changed to a lower level, until we began to run between chalk cuttings. We were nearly there now and my mother prepared to descend from the train.

It drew up with a squealing of brakes, and a hissing of steam. We climbed down, carrying our one piece of luggage, a basket with a picnic lunch in it, and I stood dumbfounded.

There was no one on the platform except for the guard of the train. I had never seen a station like this. There were no posters, no trolleys, no litter bins, no milk churns! Furthermore, once the train had pulled away, everything was still and quiet.

Before me, on a green bank, sheltered from the wind, primroses were growing, and somewhere, high above, birds were singing, which I learnt soon after were skylarks, indigenous to this chalky North Downs country.

We crossed by a footbridge, our footsteps echoing hollowly, to the up platform. Here things were much more station-like to my eyes. There was a shirt-sleeved porter, metal posters advertising Waverley pens and Nestlé's milk. There was even a chocolate machine where a penny would buy a bar of the delicious stuff.

The porter took our tickets and pointed out the way to our destination. It led across the station yard, through a gate, and on to a footpath beside a wood.

The train by now was well inside the tunnel beneath the North Downs on its way to Knockholt

station. The peace of a spring morning enveloped us as we climbed the gentle slope, the wood on our right, and the deep railway cutting on our left.

We were both glad to stop now and again to have a rest. My mother had been ill, which was the main reason for our move, and I too had not long recovered from a bout of the Spanish influenza which had plagued Europe at the end of the First World War.

The wood gave way to fields of springy turf which made a pleasant resting place. There was a sturdy black metal sign set just inside the wires separating the railway property from our path. It said:

Trespassers will be fined £2.

It seemed a pity, as already a few early blue violets could be seen there. However, there was enough to enchant us on this side of the fence.

Tiny plants, which I should recognise later as sheep's-bit scabious and thyme, were being pressed under my legs. The larks were in joyous frenzy above. The sky was blue, the now distant wood misty with early buds, and the air was heady to a London child.

A great surge of happiness engulfed me. This is where I was going to live. I should learn all about birds and trees and flowers. This is where I belonged. Any qualms about a new school vanished in these surroundings.

This was the country, and I was at home there.

It was a knowledge that was to stay throughout my life.

The Village School

Two days later, my mother took me to the
village school to be admitted as a pupil.

It was a rainy morning and I wore my new
mackintosh. In those days, little girls had a garment,
rather like Red Riding Hood's in shape, consisting of a
rubber cape with a hood. The latter could be drawn up
round the head and had a minuscule frill all round
one's face. Those mackintoshes certainly kept out the
rain, which is more than you can say for some of our
present-day raincoats, but they were airless and hot.

It was almost a mile and a quarter
to the school, along a lane already
showing a few yellow coltsfoot
and celandine flowers on the
banks, and a thickening of
buds on some large and
ancient trees which I soon
discovered were elm
and walnut.

We passed an ivy-
covered farmhouse

called Julian Brimstone Farm. There was a large yard beside it, and a wall of flint and brick separated it from the road. We paused for a minute to admire the rain-pocked pond where ducks and geese were busy about their affairs.

The stables were being cleaned out, steam rising from the dung. The few cart horses were out at work in the fields.

We passed the church on our left, standing well back from the road. A row of lime trees led to it. Then the lane passed under a splendid row of ancient elm trees, sloped gently downhill, and we were in the village street.

The first building on the right was a cream-painted shed. This was the Fire Station and housed, I learnt later, a small machine which could be pushed along by hand and trundled to any local outbreak of fire. Rumour had it that, on one of the rare occasions when it was used, the hose was found to be perished and spouted water freely all along its length, and not from the nozzle.

The small building was well embedded in a hawthorn hedge, which no doubt offered sanctuary to many a nesting bird.

Almost opposite stood a flint cottage where there lived a German couple called Ulrich. He was something of an artist and designed the black and white drawing on the parish magazine showing St Martin's church.

There were three shops on the right hand side, and

a public house called 'The Five Bells' where our lane met another. And here I had my first view of my new school.

I could not believe my eyes. Where was the great three-storey building of red brick? Where was the vast expanse of playground?

Here before me was a one-storey building with a slate roof. Steps led up to the small playground, and a row of pollarded lime trees towered above the railings. On climbing the steps we could then see some sturdy wooden benches set under the trees.

The first door had BOYS written above it, so we went round the building to the back, and entered by a door marked GIRLS. Presumably 'Mixed Infants' used this door too.

It was very quiet in the lobby, and there was no one to be seen. My mother knocked on the glass of a nearby door, and a pleasant young woman came out and said that if we would wait a moment she would tell the headmaster that we were there.

A *headmaster*? I was appalled. At my old school, we saw no male teachers, and the ruler of that distant world had been Miss Pope, a headmistress of great dignity. I had heard my Aunt Rose speak of her with due deference, and now and again she entered our classrooms and we all stood up respectfully. It was she who took assembly in the morning, and gave us important pieces of instruction such as urging us each to bring a handkerchief, or telling us that the Great War had ended which was why the Union Jack was flying from the flag-pole.

But a *headmaster*! Did this mean that boys and girls would all be mixed together, as in my Infants' days? I peered through the glass of the classroom door, and there indeed were boys and girls, much about my age, sitting in desks, although it seemed that two boys appeared to share a desk, and two girls another, so that at least one would have the comfort of sitting beside a *girl* evidently, and not a *boy*.

While we waited in the lobby among the damp coats and hats, a little girl emerged from another door and skipped up to the wash basin. There were two basins, but one was broken, and remained so, I remember, for months. There was a brass tap which gave only cold water, and this little imp set about washing her hands with a piece of yellow Sunlight soap, grey and grainy with age.

We smiled at each other. My first encounter with one of my schoolfellows cheered me.

'Hullo,' she said. 'Miss Smiff sent me out.' It sounded as though she might be in disgrace, but she showed no sign of distress. In fact, she hummed cheerfully as she endeavoured to create a lather, and then wiped her hands on a damp towel hanging nearby.

She beamed again. 'Goodbye! Got to get back,' she volunteered, and skipped back to her classroom, as Mr Clarke the headmaster appeared and beckoned us in.

He was a squarely-built man of medium height, with dark eyes and black hair. His voice was pleasant, his expression kind. I liked him at once.

We went through the classroom of the first teacher we had met, and were introduced to her. She was Miss Ellis, and smiled nicely. I was very conscious of many eyes behind me, no doubt examining me from hair to toes.

In the headmaster's room, beyond the glass and pine partition, more eyes watched us. Here the boys and girls were older, some almost grown up, it seemed to me. The oldest must have been a venerable fourteen.

Mr Clarke began to write down the particulars of my age, past schooling and so on, and my mother went through the usual ritual of spelling our surname S-H-A-F-E, which always flummoxed new acquaintances.

Meanwhile, I gazed about the room, noting a fine open fire protected by a cage-like fireguard. Along its brass top, a row of knitted gloves steamed gently.

There were some large wooden cupboards, and one glass-fronted one with an interesting-looking collection of books. (They turned out to be remarkably dreary, as it happened.) The windows were high, but a few fish-paste jars stood on the windowsills, holding early primroses and violets.

In this room, too, each desk held two children of the same sex. Exercise books were open before them, and pens were in hand, but naturally work was suspended while my mother and I were there to be scrutinised.

At length, the headmaster took us to the door,

telling Miss Ellis, in passing, that I should be in her class.

This time, we went through the boys' lobby, said our farewells to Mr Clarke, descended the steps to the village street, and began the long walk home.

I wonder now why I was not left there that day, but there must have been some good reason. In any case, it was very pleasant to have a few hours' breathing space, and to mull over in my mind the first impressions of this extraordinary place which bore no resemblance to my idea of a school.

'Do you think you will like it?' my mother asked when we were halfway home.

'Yes,' I said with conviction.

I suspect, on looking back, that she had some doubts about the type of education I should receive there. She too was accustomed to the ways of large town schools, and knew from her teacher sister Rose the high standards of attainment expected from the pupils, and the relentless pressure kept up to ensure scholastic success. Payment-by-results was not all that far behind in the teaching profession in those days, and class teachers were on their mettle to prove their worth.

I had plenty to think about. I remembered those watching eyes, boys', alarmingly strange, as well as girls'. There was not one person among them that I knew. No Aunt Rose would be with me as a protector, either on the long journey to school and back, or in that queer quiet little building I had just left. And my sister, too, was now far away.

I should be alone, and a stranger, in a completely different world.

Facing the Unknown

OPPOSITE Julian Brimstone Farm stood a pair of farm cottages, and in one of them lived a young family called Whitehead. The father worked for the local farmer, not the one who lived at Julian Brimstone Farm, but a much larger landowner whose acres lay on the other side of the road. One of his fields was opposite our own house.

Incidentally, it was in this field one day in the late twenties that I heard a little boy walking round the edge, rattling a tin with stones in it and singing hoarsely:

> O all you blackytops
> Keep off my master's crops
> Here I come
> With my big gun
> La-la-la-la-la-la.

He could not have been more than nine years of age.

Dan Whitehead was fair, of ruddy complexion and

cheerful. His wife was tall with very dark eyes and black hair, a handsome woman.

She agreed very kindly to my mother's request that her daughter Hilda might 'look after me' on the journey to and from school, at least for the first few days. We became firm friends.

Her little brother Billy was too young then to come to school, but Hilda had had her share of minding children and was conscientious in looking after me. I was exceedingly glad of her company.

I got to know that mile-and-a-quarter journey very well, for I made it four times a day. In that first spring it was Hilda who showed me where the beds of violets grew, some white and sweet-smelling, some dog violets of blue, and one rare bed of pink ones whose whereabouts we kept secret.

She also showed me a blackbird's nest near her gate not far from a patch of snowberries whose white globes enchanted us later in the year.

Every morning we called at Hilda's grandmother's house, one of a pair of clapboarded cottages a little further along the lane. I was rather afraid of the old lady, for although she was kind, and later invited us to pick gooseberries in an old overgrown orchard at the end of her garden, she had an appalling cough, and looked so ill when caught in one of its paroxysms that I feared she would die in front of me.

Hilda took all this in her stride, and we collected there a small boy called Kenneth who was being fostered in the house.

In her grandmother's scullery was a fascinating green globe which stood in a jar of water. According to the old lady, it was a weather gauge, but I never understood how it worked.

Kenneth, like Shakespeare's schoolboy, 'crept unwillingly to school', and Hilda had to use all her wiles to get him there. We also collected a younger cousin of Hilda's on the way, so that we were quite a little band as we approached the village.

Between us, on our journey, we made wonderful discoveries. A robin had built a nest on a ledge inside a hollow damson tree, near the young cousin's house. A blackbird had another tucked among a tangle of honeysuckle, at the top of a steep bank. Luckily, it was close to a telegraph pole, which helped our climbing efforts on the way to inspect the nest. Good children that we were, we did not touch the eggs, but Hilda, experienced and wise, warned us not to tell any of 'the big boys'.

'They are *cruel*!' she assured us. 'I've seen some of them throw the little birds on the road and *stamp* on them!'

We were suitably horrified, and swore never to tell of our discoveries.

About halfway to school stood a great pile of grey flints ready for road mending. This, of course, we climbed and ran along, enjoying a heady glimpse of the fields beyond the top of the hedge.

Opposite, in that first year, there was a field of sage. I had never seen more than a wispy sprig or two in London gardens, and to see and smell a whole fieldful was an amazing experience.

Between the sage field and the church stood a splendid Georgian house called Court Lodge, but even more intriguing to us children was the lodge at its gates, for in the garden of this house stood a high pole to which was fixed a length of wire which ran to the roof of the house. It was my first introduction to a wireless aerial.

Later, we had one in our own garden, and a crystal set in the sitting-room, with headphones to listen to the crackling, and occasional voice, which emerged miraculously from all the paraphernalia.

A pretty girl, called Elsie, lived at the lodge and frequently joined our party on the way to school. She had curly auburn hair, and was in Mr Clarke's class. As she also told us something about the hallowed wireless set in her home, she was obviously treated with respect.

By this time, we were almost in the village and as we entered 'The Street', as the local people called it, we could see knots of children approaching from other directions. All were on foot. I don't remember even a bicycle being ridden by a child to school, and school buses, of course, were far in the future.

Some walked from Well Hill, a mile or so north of the village, some from an outpost to the west. A few came from scattered cottages on the road from the station. Miss Smith herself, the kindly ruler of the Infants' class for many years, came by train, and walked the lonely mile from there every school morning and back in the afternoon, in rain or shine.

Most of the houses in the village itself had children living in them. Some of the families were large. There were eight or nine offspring in one cottage close to the school, and a good many parents had four or five children.

As the school bell began to ring, the Divalls and Martins emerged from their houses near Groom's, the baker; the Sparrowhawks from theirs near Neal's, the grocers; Margaret Smith from the Post Office; Harold and Violet Smith (no relation, incidentally) from a

23

handsome clapboard house, and the Wickendens from another nearby.

By the time the bell stopped, almost a hundred children had assembled. Mr Clarke appeared in the

playground, lines were formed, and boys and girls, aged from five to fourteen, entered the lobbies to start another day.

On my first morning, it was soon apparent that this school bore no resemblance to my old one.

There, we had assembled for morning prayers in an enormous hall. Miss Pope had stood on a dais, resplendent in an ankle-length dove-grey frock, with a watch pinned over her heart, and a Bible on the table before her. After singing the hymn and saying prayers, we all sat cross-legged on the floor to listen to

a story from the Bible, and to
take heed of any notices given
out before returning to our
classrooms. One of the staff
played a march on the piano
and we did our best to keep
in time as we stomped away.

Here, Mr Clarke stood
in the doorway of the partition which divided standards
one, two, three and four from
standards five, six and seven,
his own class. Miss Ellis sat at
the piano hard by, and we sang a
hymn, following the words from some rather scruffy
hymn books which we had to share. The Infants, it
seemed, attended to their devotions in their own
classroom.

Prayers were said with bowed heads, Mr Clarke
told us that he expected less noise in the playground
than he had heard yesterday, the door was closed, and
we sat down in our desks, ready for a Scripture lesson.
Now I had time to look about me, as Miss Ellis began
the story of Joseph and his brothers.

There was a large photograph
of Queen Mary and King George V
behind Miss Ellis's desk. He was
ablaze with medals and decorations,
a fine upstanding figure with a neat
beard. His Queen was wasp-waisted

in white lace, a star on her breast, her hair crisply waved. They were a handsome pair, I thought, and I was proud that my father had fought for them in France in the Royal Horse Artillery.

A large marmalade-coloured cupboard stood beside the photograph, and on its side hung a little board headed 'Attendance'. This was divided into five, one section for each school day of the week. One of the big boys from standard seven, I was to discover, came round in the morning and afternoon to count heads and to put the total on this little board.

There was a large open fire surrounded by a sturdy fireguard. I could feel its warmth from my seat in a front desk, shared with a little girl introduced to me as Rose.

Our desk was old and heavily scarred. It had two inkwells, one let into the middle and the other at the end. A groove ran from one to the other, and in it rested our pens, with lovely orange wooden holders. Mine had a new nib. Rose's had seen some wear.

There was a large blackboard propped on an easel, and Miss Ellis's chalk rested in a groove on the cross-bar of this. When the Scripture lesson was over, she began to put up some addition and subtraction sums in hundreds, tens and units, and these I found I could do, although with some difficulty. Arithmetic was not my strong point, but my early schooling carried me through, and the fact that I knew my tables inside out concealed the knowledge that this was about all I did know of the subject.

At playtime I rushed to find Hilda. Rose accompanied us, and Margaret from the Post Office was friendly, and showed me the gap where her tooth had just come out. I much appreciated the honour, and tried to hide my horror at the sight.

It was after play that my first problem arrived.

'Take out your writing books,' said Miss Ellis. She handed me a brand new one, and then turned to the blackboard.

I forget what she wrote but whatever it was, it was inscribed in copperplate. I could not read it, let alone copy it. At my old school, we had been taught to print—'to do script', as it was called—with each letter separate from the next.

I watched Rose dip in her pen and start to copy the elaborate rigmarole. Despair engulfed me.

'Get on, dear,' said Miss Ellis.

'I can't,' I faltered. 'I've only done script!'

'We done that in the Infants,' said an insufferable boy in the next row.

'When we had pencils,' contributed another smug child.

Miss Ellis took charge, and ushered me to her desk with my pristine writing book. Every eye was upon us.

'Just show me how you write,' she said encouragingly, and waved towards the incomprehensible scribble on the board.

'I can't read it,' I confessed, now near to tears.

'It says: "March comes in like a lion and goes out like a lamb." You can use my inkwell.'

I did so, and standing at her desk printed the sentence in my best script.

As I finished, the door opened and in came Mr Clarke. Miss Ellis rose and the two had a whispered conversation above my head.

Mr Clarke took up my book.

'She can't do real writing,' said the insufferable boy smugly.

'But you can read every word,' retorted Mr Clarke, 'which is more than I can say about your scrawl!'

I loved him from that moment.

Settling Down

Looking back, I now realise how lucky I was to arrive in Chelsfield at just that time.

Although the village was only seventeen miles from Charing Cross, and a mere two miles from the main London to Hastings road, it remained a close-knit rural community.

Most of the wage-earners worked on the farms, although two or three fine houses, such as Court Lodge, provided domestic employment for several more. There were two bakeries in the village and a grocer's shop, and these too had one or two local men acting as indoor helpers or drivers of the delivery vans. One baker still delivered his bread in a high gig, with a spanking bay horse to draw it.

It was a fruit-growing area, strawberries being one of the main crops. Gooseberries and raspberries also did well, and later in the year the orchards produced

excellent apples, pears and plums. There were no hops grown in our village, but extensive hop fields were cultivated some miles south towards the Weald of Kent.

Our school holidays were sensibly adapted to the seasons, for as well as short holidays at Christmas and Easter, we had a three-week fruit-picking holiday in early July, and a three-week hop-picking holiday in September. It was this acknowledgement of Nature's importance and its direct influence on rural economy which gave me such delight.

The seasons, when I lived in London, had small effect on one's life. Certainly, clothes had to be warmer in winter, the muffin man rang his bell, and the coal cart was a regular feature of the winter scene, just as the water cart, with its sprinkler, was a sign of summer. But in a town school, one was hardly aware of the change of the seasons. Holidays came at Christmas and Easter, and the main one in August when our family went to Walton-on-the-Naze to stay with my grandparents, and to share the windswept beach with other children also on holiday.

I relished the change to breaks in July and September when the country was full of interest. Shabby

August, with its drying grass and end-of-summer feeling, might just as well be spent in school where I grew increasingly happy.

My early fears, particularly of the boys, whose company had virtually vanished when I became a Big Girl at the age of six in my old school, now disappeared. It was true that they teased me, but I could take that cheerfully, used as I was to my father's bantering ways. In any case, I soon found that the girls were very motherly, and would rush to the assistance of any young thing being persecuted.

On the whole, they were a well-mannered pleasant set of children whose parents would not brook disrespect, disobedience or bad language. Most of us went either to the parish church of St Martin's or to the Wesleyan chapel which stood opposite the school. Mr Clarke, the kindest of men, nevertheless stood no nonsense from his pupils, and the cane stood in readiness for those whose behaviour merited its attention. All of us knew our limits, and if we were foolish or bold enough to kick over the traces, we knew what was in store. It all contributed to a peaceful and well-ordered society.

I might well have been bullied for I was definitely the odd one, a lone stranger amidst these closely-knit children, many of whom had known each other from birth. Apart from their general good nature and my own resilience, I unwittingly found another way to make friends.

On my previous birthday, I had been given a

scooter which I loved dearly. It was a
simple affair of a wooden platform
and an upright wooden column
which sprouted two handles. With
one's left foot on the platform and
one's right foot pushing energetically
at the ground, a fair turn of speed
could be enjoyed. Downhill, of course,
it was utter bliss, and my sister,

who also had one, demonstrated this by standing on
her scooter at the top of the hill outside our house, and
rushing down the steep quarter of a mile to the main
London road, without needing to put a foot to the
ground. We played this game down the steep slope of
the North Downs until our parents discovered it and
forbade us to go right to the traffic at the bottom so
that, much to our chagrin, we were obliged to put our
feet down some fifty yards short of our target.

At the head of the hill, opposite our house, was a
notice board which warned carters about the steepness

of the hill before them, and exhorting them not to attempt it unless 'with a properly adjusted skidpan'.

I think our right shoes acted as our skidpans for they were always worn through well before the left ones.

Miss Ellis gave me permission to bring my scooter to school, and I pounded along in fine style, little thinking of the effect it would have on my schoolfellows.

I had made the journey alone that morning, and as soon as I rattled into the village I was surrounded by admiring children. The boys were particularly interested and asked deferentially if they could 'have a go'. They took turns in scooting up and down the pavement below the school wall, while I sat on the steps and watched.

The school bell rang whilst the fun continued. When it stopped, the boys lugged it up the steps for me, begging me to let them have turns again at playtime. My star was certainly in the ascendant, and I was in the rare position of being able to state my terms.

As it happened, my scooter was banned from the playground, although I was allowed to keep it in an obscure corner of the lobby, and ride it to and from school. Needless to say, I had an accompaniment of entreating schoolfellows whenever I had my scooter with me.

In my early days at Chelsfield School, my scooter was hard-worked, partly, I suspect, because of the influence it gave me over my schoolfellows, but also because that summer of 1921 was one of endless sunshine and, consequently, quite severe drought.

I remember a straw hat which my mother made me wear. It was a boater shape, with a ribbon band of pale pink with pale blue spots. The ends hung down behind, a little longer than my hair (with fringe), and streamed behind as I scorched along on my trusty scooter. The hat was anchored by elastic under the chin.

My cotton frocks were cut in Magyar style, the short sleeves cut in one with the straight front and back, and a scooped or squared neckline. These, no doubt, were run up by my dressmaker aunt, dear Aunt Jess, whom I had left behind at 267 Hither Green Lane with Grandma Read.

These cotton frocks had knickers to match which was considered very avant-garde by my contemporaries. That summer I wore no socks, just leather sandals, the right one soon becoming dilapidated by friction with the gritty road. I don't think I ever realised the freedom of loose, light clothing so much as I did in that scorching summer. As a small child, I had worn a vest, chemise, petticoat, knickers, frock and pinafore. It was wonderful to have shed so many superfluous layers.

One would have thought that with so much clothing discarded by my mother, that over-powering hat would have gone the same way. But, in those days, heads seem to have been considered particularly vulnerable to weather in all its variety, so hats were deemed absolutely essential. Most of my school-friends sported plain linen affairs, which I thought very smart and practical. But as my own large straw was much admired by quite big girls of ten or more, I grew fonder of it in time.

Most of the girls in that hot summer wore frocks made of cotton check gingham or flowered print, but knickers were mostly white with elastic at waist and leg, although a few children still wore white cotton drawers buttoned on to a Liberty bodice. Pinafores too were still worn by one or two girls, and in the March of my arrival when winter clothes were the rule, white pinafores, black stockings and laced-up black boots were the accepted wear by some of the girls.

Hair was worn long, either in plaits or drawn back and tied up in a bow on the crown of the head. A little later, the 'American Bob' hairstyle became the thing, a great saving in hair ribbons and celluloid hair-slides which were always getting lost or broken.

The boys of my age were in shorts, usually of grey flannel, and jerseys with collars, shirt-style. In the hot weather, they wore short-sleeved cotton shirts. I much admired their striped belts which fastened with a snake's-head buckle.

Those elderly gentlemen of thirteen and fourteen in Mr Clarke's class were clad in long trousers, some I suspect, adapted from their fathers' cast-offs.

What with long trousers, breaking voices, and such important duties as counting heads morning and afternoon, not to mention collecting traysful of inkwells, it is no wonder that we small fry beyond the partition looked upon them as practically Mr Clarke's contemporaries.

They were held in some respect, and on the whole were a good influence on us younger ones. Within a year or so, they would be out in the world, the majority following their fathers into agricultural work, but some to take up work in carpenters' shops or garages. One or two would go into the Army, but very few would go on to higher education.

I cannot recall any boy winning a scholarship to the local grammar school. Times were still hard after the 1914–18 war, and were to become harder still as the Depression approached. Agriculture was in a sad way, and most country families needed every penny that could be brought in by their wage-earners. The boys themselves seemed ready and eager at fourteen to get out into the world, and as far as one could see, had no regrets about abandoning 'school-learning'.

They were not great readers although the girls seemed to be. When they left school, the latter would probably find their chief relaxation in books borrowed, as likely as not, from the splendid libraries which Kent County Council provided very early. Our family had particular cause to be grateful for this excellent service for we were all avid readers, and paid a weekly visit to the Reading Room to rummage through the library box for new treasures.

One of my library books, *Twelve Stories and a Dream* by H. G. Wells, I remember particularly vividly as Tony, our adored mongrel dog, chewed it up and we were obliged to pay some horrific sum—I think it was four shillings—for its replacement.

Our school library was poor. One or two adventure stories by Henty and R. L. Stevenson seemed to be the boys' sustenance, and I believe Louisa M. Alcott was provided for us girls. But almost all of one of the three shelves was taken up by a row of identical grey-covered books with the title *Thrift*. They must have been presented to the school by some earnest society intent on educating the poor, but in fact they were as grey inside as out, completely unreadable, and fit only for the pulping machine.

Mr Clarke was generous in lending books from his own shelves, and I recall ploughing through his copy of *David Copperfield* which my mother insisted must be shrouded in brown paper, whilst in my care, to protect it.

We had one or two readers in our desks, mostly composed of extracts from Goldsmith, Shakespeare, Scott and the like. There was a dearth of humorous writing, and very little poetry. Most of the latter was learnt by rote in the lower junior classes under Miss Ellis's supervision, and I suspect that the school leavers, as a whole, had only these remnants to cheer them through life.

In Mr Clarke's class, we were given a poetry book occasionally, and told to learn a poem. Some of the girls did this conscientiously, and I know that I learnt Walter de la Mare's enchanting poem 'Nod' at that time. It is with me still.

To test our poetical knowledge, Mr Clarke sometimes called out a child at random to recite. The boys, to a man, reeled off that rather dreadful poem of Wordsworth's:

> The cock is crowing
> The stream is flowing
> The small birds twitter
> The lake doth glitter (etc.)

which they had been compelled to learn years earlier. Somehow, they always got away with it, and we girls, who had been industrious, were rightly incensed.

But when it came to singing, the school came into its own. We were well drilled in Tonic Solfa, the narrow strip of shiny material draped over the blackboard and our teacher's red-tipped pointer bounding up and down from Doh-to Soh-to Doh while we sang to its demands.

Mr Clarke had a superb bass voice, almost as velvety dark as Paul Robeson's, and led us surely through the intricacies of *The National Song Book*, with Miss Ellis accompanying on the piano.

We really enjoyed singing lessons, and probably our favourite was 'Charlie Is My Darling', for we were all impressed by one of the big boys who was kind, good-looking and already a charmer, and whose name was Charlie.

We sang it with all the fervour of youthful admiration rather than ardour for the Jacobite cause. And if Mr Clarke knew what lay behind our fortissimo rendering, as surely he did, he gave no sign.

Exploring

THE Easter holiday brought my sister Lil home for good, much to our mutual pleasure.

Unlike some sisters separated by three years in age, we always got on well together. Naturally, we had our fights too. Lil was much cleverer than I was in these encounters, and one of her subtlest moves, when I was about five and had just mastered garter stitch, was to do a row of purl knitting on my plain-knitted doll's scarf. Powerless to unravel it, and yet loathing this wrong line in my painfully-acquired inch of work, I could only yell with rage—or I may have bitten her. I was rather good at biting when young.

Occasionally we had fights over our dolls, usually if we were playing schools with them. They sat in a row, usually propped against the fender, and were

given arithmetic tests set, I need hardly say, by Lil. We were supposed to 'do' our own dolls' papers, and as Lil's mathematical ability was always outstanding, and mine just the opposite, my poor charges invariably failed, and Lil's succeeded brilliantly.

However, I retaliated later by jumping out unexpectedly, preferably in darkness, from handy cupboards or corners, and frightening my sister into quaking terror. I found this ruse very satisfactory.

During those first summer months, we explored our new surroundings, enjoying each other's company after our brief separation.

The garden was still in the making. Flower beds were being dug by my father, and a vegetable patch. A tennis court was also laid out, and one or two chicken houses complete with runs were set up.

My father, in common with a lot of men after the war, was deluded enough to imagine that a small fortune could be made from chicken-farming. He soon found that it was one of the quickest roads to penury, but at least we always had plenty of eggs to eat.

But it was outside our garden gate that we found most of our excitement.

There was a roadside pond almost opposite our house. In the early spring it was awash with frogs' spawn, I was to discover, but even now, in April, it had its charms. Trees grew around three sides, mostly scrubby hawthorns, but there was one large tree, probably a crab apple or wild cherry, which we could climb. Here we found a perch, and watched the occasional passer-by who had no knowledge of his hidden and delighted watchers.

The pond was not large enough to harbour moorhens or mallard, but homely birds like blackbirds and starlings, or a flutter of squabbling little tabby sparrows, came to drink and splash in the shallows, and we were entranced.

Halfway down the steep hill, a cart track led off which ended in a south-facing field heavily hedged. These hedges yielded more joy, for under them grew sheets of blue violets, many of them sweet-smelling, and a little later spangles of white stitchwort whose seedpods could be popped with great satisfaction.

One hedge was composed of bullace bushes, that round pale green wild fruit which is scarce these days.

Later that year, we picked basketsful of these little plums, and made pounds of scarlet jelly, sharp to the taste, which made a welcome addition to the larder shelves.

During that summer we discovered wild strawberries, dog roses, honeysuckle, bryony, wild hops and scores of other delights in that field, some appealing to taste, or scent, or simply enchanting the eye with colour and form.

But even more exciting was the wood which lay beyond it. It was one of those pleasant and welcoming oak and hazel woods, now becoming rare, giving way as they have to the sinister conifer plantations to be seen dominating so much of our countryside.

Our wood was light. The sunshine shone through the leaves upon clumps of primroses, and later the sea of bluebells whose scent was everywhere.

Underfoot, the ground was soft with the leaf mould of centuries. Plenty of rabbits burrowed here, or skittered away at our approach with a glimpse of white scuts. Now and again, a squirrel could be seen leaping airily, a puff of grey smoky fur, in the branches overhead. And always there were birds. Wood pigeons clattered from the oak trees, blackbirds fled squawking from the bramble bushes, tits collected the swinging caterpillars from their gossamer threads to carry to their young, and scores of birds unseen rustled among the dead leaves or stirred the young bracken.

Every visit to the wood brought fresh discoveries. In one clearing, a gigantic beech tree grew on a sandy slope. This provided massive low branches, grey and crinkled like elephant skin, upon which we sat, bouncing up and down with the wind in our hair.

We found a yew tree not far away which soon became our particular headquarters. It was easy to climb, and we would sit aloft in its aromatic fastness, picking at the trunk to uncover its pink fleshiness, and relishing the comfort of its rough support and the glossy beauty of its foliage.

Sometimes we brought our dolls to enjoy the pleasures of the wood. We would make diminutive jellies or tiny sandwiches for them, and give them a picnic in some particularly favoured glade. Tony, the dog, always accompanied us although he resented being left below the trees we climbed, and mooched about, whining pathetically at being deserted.

On one occasion, when my sister and I and another

little friend called Peggy were taking our ease, high in the yew tree, there was the crack of an air gun, and Tony, far below, began yelping in terror.

As one man, yelping ourselves, we crashed down through the branches, knickers, Liberty bodices, skirts, hair, all drawn upwards, to confront a startled man with a light gun. He was looking white and shaken, as well he might, at the sight of three such vociferous little girls.

'You ought to look at what you're shooting at!' screamed Peggy, scarlet-faced, and the superbly un-grammatical sentence, and its intonation, has stayed with me over the years.

Tony was engulfed in our loving embraces. There was a slight smear of blood on his chest where the pellet had grazed him, but this did not stop the dog from making the most of his troubles, and I remember

we took turns in carrying him home, after berating the man soundly, threatening him with police, fathers, the RSPCA and any other relevant authority we could call to mind.

Tony lay on his back, his four legs stiffly in the air, as we bore him homeward. He weighed a ton, and after having disinfectant dabbed on his wound, recovered immediately at the sight of his dinner plate.

Looking back now, some sixty-odd years on, I suppose the man had been out to get a rabbit for the larder, saw a movement and took a pot shot. The sudden descent of three wrathful children, falling from the heavens, must have made him glad that he had not let fly at a pigeon, or any other animal near our lofty perch. He was certainly a very frightened man.

The pond, the hazel wood, the fields and hedgerows provided us with a thousand marvels. An old chalk-pit, across a nearby field, gave us endless pleasure as we slid down the slopes to the detriment of our clothes. Downland country is always at its best in summer, and that never-to-be-forgotten spell of brilliant sunshine, week after week, gilded the long outdoor days, burnished our town-bred limbs, bleached our hair, and illumined our memories for ever.

Only streams were lacking in that part of the North Downs, but later we found the thrill of running water when we walked to Shoreham in the Darent valley, some four miles away, the village immortalised by Samuel Palmer. Later still, as we grew older, bolder and stronger, we explored more of those lovely villages, Otford, Brasted and Chevening, carrying our picnic lunches, and bringing home the gold of kingcups, exotic trophies from a foreign land.

A Reluctant Musician

URING that summer term, Lil and I went to school together. I don't think the impact made upon my sister was very great. For one thing, she only spent one term there, and I spent ten.

But there was another reason. Her thoughts were of the school ahead, and the results of the examination which she had sat recently. These obligatory weeks at the village school were of a temporary nature, and although the respite from town pressures must have been welcome, the school and its children were not to affect her as keenly as they did me.

News came during that term that she had been given a place at Blackheath High School, and the family rejoiced. Naturally, there was a great deal of preparation to be done, and there was a flurry of shopping for school uniform, black stockings, name

tapes, shoe bags, a satchel, and so on. Although I was proud of her achievement, I was secretly glad that I was spared all this bother.

The biggest worry of all was how Lil was to get to this new school from Chelsfield. At that time, there was no bus along the main Hastings road to London and trains did not fit in. It was necessary to get to Farnborough where a 47 bus could be caught.

This was a good three miles from home, and mostly uphill. She would have to make the journey twice daily by bicycle as well as the bus trip. It meant a very early start in the mornings, which was not too awful in the summer, but the winter trips were formidable.

The fear of traffic and the fear of child molesters were minimal in those happier days, but my parents soon realised that the journey was really too much for a young girl, particularly as home-work increased. In the end, Lil was transferred to a school in Bromley, a much more accessible place which could be reached by train, and later by bus.

Meanwhile, I settled happily to my carefree life. By now I had made several good friends. Besides Hilda, I relished the company of Margaret from the

Post Office and particularly that of Norah Foreman whose father was a fruit farmer at Well Hill.

These friends sometimes came to tea, or I went to their homes, where we inspected each other's toys, exchanged books, dressed each other's dolls, or simply enjoyed the strange pleasures of a different house and garden.

My parents too began to make friends as soon as the early settling-in process was over. They both joined the church choir and the local Glee Club. Both were musical, and sang well, and my father had played the organ at church from the age of about fourteen or so. It was no wonder that they had insisted on piano lessons for their daughters at an early age when we lived in London.

My sister must have been eight or nine when these began, and she took to it like a duck to water. I, three years younger, went along with her and had the basics taught me. I loathed it.

These lessons took place in a house quite near our own at Lewisham, and I only remember a rather stuffy room with a circular sofa, covered in red plush, where I sat whilst Lil practised scales, arpeggios and the advanced end of Ezra Read's musical exercises. Needless to say, I hardly reached Page 3.

When we moved, I had hoped fondly that this torture would cease. Lil was to continue her musical studies at school, and it was my hope that any ambitions for me in that line would die a natural death.

However, a music teacher gave lessons in the

village, and I was signed on. A more reluctant pupil poor Miss Hill never had.

She seemed to me a very old lady, small and afflicted with a spinal disability. She looked after her father, a handsome old gentleman who was probably then in his seventies, so that his daughter was probably then only in her forties.

She dressed in dark clothes and wore a gold chain and spectacles. She was exceedingly kind and patient, but kept a ruler at hand for tapping erring fingers. I knew that ruler well.

I progressed slowly and painfully through Ezra Read and can still play 'Sweet Memories' (to the mental accompaniment of Miss Hill's ruler). After that, new works were bought, one by one, and as they had to be sent for and despatched by post, I soon learnt a major delaying tactic.

There was something called Continental Fingering which showed the notes with 1, 2, 3, 4 or 5 above them. This, I professed, was impossible for me to follow, and I stuck out for English Fingering—always the patriot—which showed the thumb as a cross, and the fingers numbered 1 to 4. This, for some reason, always took longer to procure, so that I could rattle away for another week or two at Ezra Read or Reger, and save myself, and Miss Hill's ruler, a good deal of unnecessary activity.

After my half-hour's ordeal, Miss Hill gave me a cup of tea and a biscuit, and once, some Edinburgh rock, which was new to me and has remained a weakness of mine ever since. I was much intrigued by a paper cut-out ball, fixed to the ceiling, which she explained was 'the flies' playground' and which kept them away from the rest of the room in theory.

I grew very fond of Miss Hill as time passed. My lessons took place after school, and she would accompany me, after our tea party, along a grassy lane by the side of her house to a footpath across strawberry fields which gave me a quick way home.

The house was beautiful, built in Queen Anne's reign, and standing high above the road, as so many houses did in that village. The garden was composed of a number of flower beds surrounded by low box hedges, and here old Mr Hill would be strolling or sitting on a garden seat. He was always well wrapped up, a white silk muffler at his throat. I was particularly impressed with the way he took off his cap to me, displaying silvery hair, and gave me a courtly little bow. Not many people treated me so politely, and I much appreciated his courtesy.

One winter afternoon of bitter cold, it began to snow. Dusk was falling, and the whirling snow flakes made it darker still. Miss Hill was much perturbed, and there was no way of getting in touch with my parents, for neither household had a telephone. I was quite game to strike out on my own, and rather looked forward to being part of the wild weather, but Miss Hill insisted on my sitting by the fire whilst she overcame the problem.

Luckily she remembered that Mr Stanley, the milkman, should be arriving, and as his farm was near my home, he would give me a lift.

I was wrapped up as carefully as a Christmas parcel, scarf arranged over my mouth and chin, and tied securely behind my back, whilst we awaited Mr Stanley.

When he came, the position was explained to him and I was welcomed on board his milk float. My music case was stuffed under a shelf at the front, Mr Stanley flicked his whip, and Miss Hill waved from the lighted doorway.

It was a blissful journey through the flurry of snow. I stood up at the front watching the flakes melt as they landed on the pony's black back. We fairly spanked along, the pony snorting and tossing his head at this strange element, and anxious to get back to a warm stable.

It was the most exciting ride I had ever had. There was nothing, I decided, to touch a milk float for perfect transport, and I was sorry when the trip ended at my gate and I had to wave goodbye to Mr Stanley.

The business of lifts to and from school I soon had organised. It began, I think, with an offer from Mr Curtis of Julian Brimstone Farm, one wet lunch time. He had been to the Post Office in his van, saw me emerging from school, and kindly ran me home through the puddles. This was such a superior alternative to the mile-and-a-quarter footslog home and back that I began to take note of regular transport which ran at times convenient to my school hours.

On Wednesdays, I was sometimes lucky enough to catch Mr Tutt's van. He was a fishmonger, and we dealt with him regularly. Occasionally, Mr Groom the baker went our way. Mr Smallwood, the other baker, drove a smart gig on his rounds, but would not be prevailed upon to give lifts. I was sorry about this, as he had a particularly handsome pony, and I should have relished a ride behind it.

But my most enjoyable lift was on Monday afternoons when the corn chandler Hodsall drove a massive cart, heavy with sacks of grain, seeds, cattle food and the like through the village just as we came out of school.

He was a slow taciturn man. Now I come to think of it, he was probably not Mr Hodsall himself, but I always thought of him so. I don't suppose we exchanged more than a dozen words during our journey. He sat, the reins slack across the great back of his cart horse, with a clay pipe upside down in his mouth.

I was content to watch the swaying back, surrounded by the wholesome smell of grain, and leaning against one of the sturdy sacks, my legs dangling from the wooden plank that served as a bench.

He pulled up outside my house without a word, getting down himself to grope under the wagon for the skidpan which hung from a chain beneath it. He took no notice of my thanks, affixed the skidpan as advised by the wooden notice on the bank, clambered up again, and set off, wordless, down the hill.

I was never a pony-mad little girl, but I loved these horses which I met now and again, and was glad that I experienced, for a short time, that fast-dying era of horse-drawn transport. Later, I was to make use of some of these memories when I began to write novels.

Accepting, or asking for, lifts from strangers was taboo, of course, and my parents made this plain, but they knew my benefactors well by this time and, knowing the pleasure I derived from my rides, they appreciated the kindness which prompted them.

Beginning to Question

WHEN I was promoted from Miss Ellis's class to the other side of the marmalade-coloured partition, I sat in a desk with Norah and was under Mr Clarke's tutelage.

At least, for most of my day I was under Mr Clarke's eye, but when our daily Arithmetic lesson occurred, I was banished to my former standard as I was so backward in the subject.

I had managed to struggle along with the four rules in hundreds, tens and units, and even in pounds, shillings and pence, thanks to my early grounding, but when awful problems about Arthur having twice as much pocket money as Gwendolin, although only a third of Ned's, I began to falter. As for dripping taps over baths, express trains passing each other, and all the rest of standard five's problems, they were far too much for me, and it was from then on that I was the despair of innumerable mathematics teachers until I was eighteen. After that, no one bothered, much to my relief.

But the rest of the day was spent in the happy company of Norah and the top classes of the school.

Mr Clarke was a cheerful man and we learned quite a lot, and Norah and I were delighted to be sharing a desk.

One day, Mr Clarke boomed at us:

> Norah and Dora
> Don't talk
> Any more-a.

which we considered the height of wit. I hope we stopped exasperating him, at least for a time, but we had so much to talk about that I am sure the chatter continued.

The school day was pretty regular. It began with prayers, then a Scripture lesson, ghastly Arithmetic, playtime, then Geography or History. Somewhere, fitted in, was a lesson called Drill, which took place in the playground and consisted of exercises done in four lines or teams. For this, the boys took off their jackets, and we girls stuffed our skirts into our knickers. No one changed footwear so that boys with iron studs in their boots skidded about rather alarmingly.

We also played ring games such as 'Twos and Threes', and sometimes rounders.

In the afternoon, on Mondays, Wednesdays and Fridays, we girls returned to Miss Ellis's care and faced Needlework. I was about as competent at this as at Arithmetic, and was usually allowed to practise different sorts of hems on a piece of unbleached calico which smelt of dog biscuits and was soon spotted with blood-pricks. Occasionally, I was given the lowly task of polishing the steel knitting needles with a limp scrap of emery paper, while my clever contemporaries tackled aprons, and handkerchief sachets, and kettle-holders. As far as I was concerned, rubbing away with my emery cloth, they were welcome.

Meanwhile, the boys were busy with something called Mechanical Drawing which involved a lot of work with rulers and pencils, copying cones and other large geometrical shapes set before them on Mr Clarke's desk. I suppose it trained their eyes and hands for some sort of future work, but it cannot have been much fun.

Once a week, we had a much freer and easier drawing and painting lesson altogether, and we were supposed to bring something to the class for our subject. The girls were usually fairly responsible and arrived bearing a rose or daffodil, or perhaps a toy or an ornament from home, on which to try their skill.

The boys invariably had forgotten to bring anything, and, as the afternoon school bell tolled, there was a mad rush to a privet bush in a nearby garden.

The irate householder invariably emerged to protest at this wholesale assault on his hedge, but by that time the boys were halfway up the school steps.

After playtime in the afternoon, things grew suitably easy, and we recited, or sang from *The National Song Book*, or had a story read to us or, better still, enjoyed something billed as Silent Reading when we could get on with our own books. It was a well-ordered life, if a trifle slow, and we were content.

Sometimes the day was enlivened by a visit from someone from the outside world. Mr Fox, one of the managers, occasionally called to see if we were all present and correct, and read our names aloud from the register. We responded with 'Here, sir.'

My name, as always, caused difficulty, and Mr Fox delighted our class by pronouncing it as 'Sharfer' on one occasion, and 'Shaffey' on another. It took some time for me to live this down.

Another manager was Mrs Richford, a kind and motherly lady who was more than welcome as she always brought a large tin of fruit drops with her. We all loved a visit from Mrs Richford.

Now and again, we had a visitor from other and more distant parts. One that I remember came to give us a lecture on the evils of DRINK, although at our age we had not met with much temptation in that line.

However, he gave us a fiery address, and hung a collection of diagrams over the blackboard which showed the result of consuming alcohol on various organs of the body. These were in colour, a horrid tangle of incomprehensible tubes, and when the picture of a drunkard's heart was displayed, one of the big boys slipped quietly under his desk in a dead faint and had to be carried into the fresh air amidst general sympathy.

I was particularly sorry as he had recently asked me to be his sweetheart, which I took to be a step towards matrimony. However, fond of him as I was, I now felt that I could not face a future with one quite so frail, and felt obliged to decline the honour, some days later, when he had completely recovered. He bore the reverse so well that I suspect that he had probably forgotten all about the offer.

I had a number of proposals about this time which, to be honest, I found rather a nuisance, especially as they seemed to come from boys I had hardly noticed before. One proposal came when I was particularly busy fishing for frogs' spawn in our pond. You know how it is when you are collecting frogs' spawn, such heavy, awkward slippery stuff, particularly if equipped with only a wobbly butterfly net and a one-pound jam jar, and I really could not give my full attention to his plea. In any case, I told him, as I struggled with my task, I really preferred Alan, and if he asked me then I should accept him.

My suitor said that he quite understood, but if I changed my mind, or

Alan did not come up to scratch (and he didn't!), then his offer still stood.

I can't help thinking that he must have grown up into a very nice man.

As quite a number of children came from a distance and could not get home to lunch and back, as I did, they brought a meal with them, for organised school dinners were many years ahead.

Once or twice, in very hot weather, I remember that I took sandwiches which my mother had prepared. They were wrapped in greaseproof paper and packed in a Palm Toffee tin, and there was usually an apple for dessert.

We were allowed on fine days to take our meal to the village recreation ground, some hundred yards away, and there to picnic, and it was on one of these occasions that I felt some shock in seeing one or two of my fellow picnickers' repasts. Two thick slices of white bread and a cube of cheese seemed to be their lot, but what really staggered me was the fact that the food was wrapped in newspaper. There were even greyish smears on the bread from the newsprint, but all was demolished with gusto, to my secret bewilderment.

More shocks awaited me. One little girl asked me

to go with her to the shop, and there she asked for 'a specked orange', which mystified me. The crate was obligingly sorted over, and an orange handed down by the shopkeeper, and the child gave a halfpenny for it.

'What is a specked orange?' I asked on our way back to school. She showed me a dark brown spot on its peel.

'But it's going bad!' I protested.

'That's why it's cheap,' she told me. 'It's specked.'

This exchange appalled me. Heaven knows we were far from rich ourselves, but my mother, who was an excellent cook, would never have allowed us to eat doubtful food, let alone set out to buy it.

This incident gave me a great deal to think about. There were obviously different standards, and the one I had grown up to accept, and never questioned until now, might not be the correct one after all. My schoolfellow had enjoyed that specked orange. She had eaten it hungrily, and even nibbled the marred skin with relish. Furthermore, she had been pleased to have bought something cheaply. The whole trans-action had given her satisfaction. Could it be that my mother was over-careful? Was a specked orange good value for a halfpenny? Was it right to reject it, as I would have done, and to have paid twice as much for a perfect orange? It was a puzzle.

Perhaps grown-ups were not always right after all.

Perils and Pastimes

THE happy months slipped by, and every one brought fresh discoveries, and I probably learnt as much on my walks to school as I did in the classroom.

Spring brought not only violets and primroses, but fleshy toothwort which I found under a cluster of elm trees. The honeysuckle put forth some of the first new leaves, and the walnut trees at Julian Brimstone Farm were auburn with young foliage.

In the summer, I discovered silverweed, its feathery foliage flat in the chalky dust at the side of the road, and its bright yellow flowers, like shallow cups, which smelt of almonds. The crab apple tree dropped small unripe fruit, no bigger than marbles, covered in grey velvet.

In the autumn came the joy of hazel nuts and walnuts, and a plenteous supply of blackberries in the hedges.

And in the winter, despite the intense cold of those windswept North Downs, there was still plenty to admire. Snow could drift into piles which hid the hedges, swirling into fantastic shapes like clouds. Holly berries and yew berries lit their dark foliage, and gave promise of Christmas.

There were hazards as well as joys on my journeys. For one thing, the geese at Julian Brimstone Farm sometimes emerged from the yard, and wandered about in the road, picking up grit or pecking at the grassy verge by the flint wall.

They strongly resented anyone passing through their territory and set up a terrible honking cacophony as I attempted to edge past them. No wonder the Romans kept them as watch dogs!

Worse still, they would pursue me, hissing malevolently, snake-like necks outstretched, eyes as cold and blue as the aquamarines in my mother's pendant. With wings flapping, they could get up a fine turn of speed and, fleeing from them one day, I fell in the gritty road and barked both knees.

My lamentations brought forth Mr and Mrs Curtis, and I was taken into the farm kitchen and given first aid. The gentle swabbing I understood, but when Mr Curtis dipped a wing feather, probably dropped by one of my adversaries, into a bottle of iodine, and stroked the fiery stuff over my wounds, it was as much as I could do to quell my shrieks and to try to appear suitably grateful.

In the summer there was another problem. Wasps liked to make their nests in the banks bordering the lane, and normally we could give them a wide berth and hurry by safely. But one day, a naughty boy who was with us, thrust a stick into the hole and stirred up the contents.

Rightfully incensed at this treatment, the wasps fizzed out of the hole and attacked us. I was wearing my mackintosh, and two or three of the monsters got inside and stung me fiercely.

I was as furious as the wasps, and we all set about the boy who had disturbed them. As far as I can remember, he had no stings at all, as you might expect in this unjust world.

But except for such mishaps as these, we were a remarkably healthy lot, and I can't remember the First Aid box at school ever being in much use.

People had far fewer potions and pills in their homes then. Our own medicine box housed only such simple things as tins of Vaseline, boracic ointment and boracic powder which was dissolved in warm water to cure eye troubles.

A large roll of pink lint for spreading on grazed knees and a few rolls of bandages in different widths, with a bottle of medical disinfectant, took up most of the room. The narrowest bandage was used to make 'dollies' on battered fingers.

A large brown jar of mixed cod liver oil and malt was a fixture in the cupboard during the winter months, and a revolting white mixture called Scotts' Emulsion stood hard by, with a picture of a fisherman with an enormous fish draped over his shoulder and down his back, on the label.

These aids to health were largely for the benefit of my sister, who suffered from coughs in the winter, but I was obliged to gulp down some of the stuff now and again. Other winter ills, such as chilblains and chapped faces, were treated with Melrose for the former, and Pond's Cold Cream for the latter.

In the summer, stings were usually dabbed with a Reckitt's blue bag, and sunburn eased with calamine lotion or witch hazel.

But, on the whole, our family and my school friends thrived in the boisterous downland air. Certainly those winters were enough to toughen up anyone, and of necessity we had plenty of exercise.

Other activities cropped up. As well as my music lessons, I was enrolled as a Brownie, and meetings took place once a week.

Our Brown Owl was a daughter of one of the big houses in the village, so that we had the run of large and well-kept grounds for learning such things as woodcraft, lighting camp fires, and recognising a variety of plants and trees.

There was a summer-house available for wet days, and here we struggled with knots, granny, reef, clove-hitch, slip and a score more whose names I forget, and whose making I never completely mastered.

I liked my uniform and the tie pinned with a brass brooch with an elf on it, to show that I was in the elf patrol. I liked playing in the grounds of the noble Queen Anne house, but I was not really an ardent Brownie and never craved a sleeveful of badges as some of my friends did, and I actively disliked squatting in a ring and making hideous noises at the beginning and end of the session.

My sister was enrolled as a Girl Guide, but as her school activities were so arduous, she soon made her escape and was, I suspect, much relieved. We were never to become great joiners of societies and clubs.

We both played tennis on the new court, still remarkably uneven and needing to be marked out with a paint brush and a bucket of whitening. Neither of us was much good, but we helped to make up a four now and again when grown-up friends came to play with my father. I was allowed to serve from the halfway line, with my eight-and-a-half ounce racket.

My sister seemed to have a great deal of homework to do, and I felt sorry for her sitting with her books spread out on the dining table and working by the light of an Aladdin lamp.

She was a conscientious child and worried if things went wrong. She told me about life at her school, the bells which rang when a lesson ended, the trek to the rooms where some specific subject was taught, such as the Art room, the Chemistry laboratory, the Geography room, the Botany room, and so on.

There was something called 'the silence rule' which forbade talking on stairs and corridors. It would never do for Norah and me, I decided. There were desk inspections, and uniform inspections, and fortnightly reviews of work completed. Marks went from A to E, instead of something out of ten as in the village school. If you had three Es in a row, it seemed that you were sent to detention—a terrible disgrace. On top of that, she had the train journey which involved changing at Orpington station, and invariably meant a wait of anything up to half an hour.

It all sounded rather daunting to me, and ominously reminiscent of the great school which I had first attended—all bustle and endeavour, and trying to do better than the next child. My village school seemed much more delightful in comparison.

My parents, I knew, had high hopes of my joining Lil when I was eleven years old. A few children at my school sat for a scholarship examination early in the year, and Margaret from the Post Office was successful, and went on to Bromley where she did very well.

My Aunt Rose did her best to encourage my educational progress by keeping me supplied with such books as *Lamb's Tales From Shakespeare*, and *Golden Legends* which contained stories from all over the world, and one particularly affecting one called 'The Children of Lir'. It was a horribly sad Irish tale about a princess who knitted vests from nettles for her brothers. I think they had been turned into swans, and this was the only way to turn them back into men. Looking back through the mists of time, I now wonder how she managed to transform nettles into knitting yarn. I found the whole thing deeply disturbing.

My parents too made valiant efforts to educate us, and we took a monthly magazine, edited by Arthur Mee, called *My Magazine*, and at the end of each year, the twelve issues were bound into one imposing volume.

It must have been somewhat exasperating for our parents to see that the first thing we turned to was a page of drawings and captions recounting the

71

adventures of the Hippo Boys who were almost as enchanting as Mrs Bruin and her pupils in *Tiger Tim's Weekly*, whose escapades I followed with rapture. However, quite a lot of general knowledge seemed to be absorbed from the more educational pages of *My Magazine* over the years, so that our parents' expenditure may have been justified after all.

When Lil was not heavily engaged in her school affairs, we still gave our dolls some attention, read voraciously, ran errands, helped our father in the garden, and our mother in the kitchen.

Occasionally we made toffee. It cost sixpence to make a meat tin full, and we bought the main ingredients at our nearest shop which was at the foot of the hill.

This village rejoiced, and still does of course, in the name of Pratts Bottom. The shop was kept then by an imposing lady called Mrs Bird.

We bought from her one pound of demerara sugar and a quarter of a pound of desiccated coconut. These two purchases took all our sixpence—the equivalent of today's two and a half pence.

Having trudged back up the hill, we put half a cup of water into a saucepan, a large lump of butter and let it melt.

Then we added the sugar and coconut and stirred assiduously. When it thickened, we turned the lovely

mess into a meat
tin, and tried to
possess our souls in
patience. Scraping the
saucepan, and rasping
the goo from the wooden
spoon with our teeth, helped
to pass the time.

Apart from the bliss of
having such an enormous
amount of sweet stuff all at once,
there was the exquisite suspense of waiting to see if it
turned out as *fudge* or *toffee*.

Either way, we were happy, and there were no
prouder cooks in the kingdom.

Work and Play

THE Women's Institute had a considerable influence on our lives in those early days at Chelsfield.

The movement had been launched nationally not many years before, and my mother joined the local branch soon after we arrived in the village in 1921.

I suspect that my father encouraged her in this. Not only was she still recovering from major surgery, and cheerful company was good for her, but used as she was to London and its ways, I think my father may have thought that she might be lonely.

Even after their marriage, she had been in close touch with her mother, sisters and brothers, and immediately before the move to Chelsfield, she had been in daily contact with the family household at 267 Hither Green Lane.

My father was away from home from early morning until the evening, at his work in an insurance office in north London. It must have been a beast of a journey, probably involving three hours, at least, of the day in tedious travelling, but I never heard him complain.

It did mean, though, that my mother was alone except for my half-hour with her at lunch time, and no doubt my father was anxious for her to make friends.

The W.I. was exactly the right place to do this and had, in fact, been founded, as everyone knows, with this as one of its main aims.

My mother took to it like a duck to water, and very soon found herself secretary, which will come as no surprise to newcomers to villages everywhere.

Besides these clerical responsibilities with which she dealt competently, she was very keen on the other activities offered, and I well remember helping her to manhandle a dreadfully awkward and heavy pouffe to the Reading Room where upholstery classes were being held.

Cookery demonstrations particularly appealed to her, and we were willing guinea-pigs when she tried out new recipes on the family. Two which I recall were Cheese Aigrettes, a sort of savoury pancake, and Portuguese Soup which had a good amount of rice and tomatoes in it, and was as sustaining as it was delicious.

Friends were soon made, some of them the mothers of my own school fellows, including Norah's mother. If my father had entertained any fears about loneliness, they must have been quickly dispelled. The change from life in London suited her.

Something of its difference was brought home to me one afternoon when Aunt Rose was visiting us, and she and my mother were talking as they reclined in deck chairs. I lay on the grass, ostensibly reading, but ears cocked to hear the conversation.

It turned on my prospects of success in the future scholarship examination. Aunt Rose took an avid interest in our school progress, and sometimes passed on a message from our last revered headmistress Miss Pope, who had taken great pride in Lil's achievements and had hoped fondly that I would emulate her.

'You see,' Aunt Rose went on to say, 'she may be *happy* enough at this school, but does she get the same *stimulation*? I mean, town life has so much more to offer. More people, more points of view, competition with other children.'

I could have told her that absence of these three things was exactly what I liked best about my new school. I remembered the throngs of people in shops, dodging others on crowded pavements, enduring the racket in a town playground.

As for the stimulation of a town scene, it ranked as way down the list compared with the joys and excitement of a country lane, or our beloved oak and hazel wood. There was much which I had actively hated in the London streets I knew, as well as the noise. I was frightened of trains thundering over bridges above my head. I was afraid of the street hawkers, rag and bone men, cats' meat men, coal men, knife-grinders, all, in fact, who bellowed their services or wares with such ferocity.

The only good point about town streets was the hoardings with their advertisements, for upon these I could practise my newly-acquired skill of reading. My favourite was one advertising Nestlé's milk, and it showed two cats, one grey striped and skinny, the other round and white. Behind them was a night sky, complete with a moon, and below them was the verse:

> The ghost of Tabby
> Fed on skim
> Is all the war
> Has left of him.
> But Nestlé's is
> Full cream to the brim.

Attractive as I found this poster, chiefly because I adored cats, it could not make up for the many horrors of travelling about London. If this was what Aunt Rose termed 'stimulation', I could do without it.

Besides, I *did* see people. There were my friends at school, the grown-ups such as Miss Hill, Mr Curtis, Mr Hodsall and Mr Stanley who were kind to me, and whose company I enjoyed. And as for aunts, uncles and cousins, they were frequent visitors and provided a certain amount of gentle competition when we played pat-ball tennis or French cricket.

Furthermore, these encounters came in small numbers, often a one-to-one confrontation, with plenty of time to spare, and peace in which to savour the relationship. I had seen hordes of children in my old school playground, and knew hardly any of them. At Chelsfield, I knew and appreciated them all.

I hope that my mother did not take her older sister's words too much to heart. (One should always take sisters' advice with a pinch of salt.) But she was ambitious for her two daughters and, as I have mentioned earlier, I think she may have wondered if my new school would give me as good an education as the old one.

She need not have worried. I may have had to go down two or three standards in Arithmetic lesson, but

my knowledge of flowers, trees, birds and animals had burgeoned, and my affection for my new friends grew as steadily as my physical well-being which flourished in this blissful country setting.

Apart from Arithmetic, I found the work at school not too arduous. Mr Clarke was not a hard taskmaster. His lessons were interesting and he encouraged questions.

He was of an equable dispostion, and I can never remember him in a rage. He had made a comfortable niche for himself in the village and lived in the school house next door. He took part in village affairs, and aired his beautiful bass voice in the church choir.

He had a pretty wife, whom we schoolchildren only saw rarely, when she was hanging out washing or doing some other job in the garden which ran along beside the boys' playground.

Their two little boys we often saw playing there, or about in the village with their mother. Sometimes they ventured into the playground when the gate in the fence between our property and theirs had been ajar. I can remember our delight when two young faces appeared at the window high above, and behind, Mr Clarke's desk.

Alerted by our mirth and inattention, he soon summed up the situation and dashed out to rescue the intruders. It was as well that he did, for they had climbed upon two or three ancient and rickety desks, lodged against the outside wall, and anyone heavier than his two toddler sons could have capsized them.

At that time, quite a lot of written work was done in our exercise books, and general neatness in handwriting was stressed far more than it is these days. Although I never mastered the copperplate writing which my fellows used, I got along pretty swiftly with my script, which now began to join up in a ham-fisted fashion rather like the Marion

Richardson style which became fashionable some ten years later.

One afternoon a week, we had Composition lesson, a session heartily disliked by most of the pupils, particularly the boys. I must admit that the subjects set were somewhat pedestrian. 'A Day At The Sea', 'Helping Mother', 'A Trip to London' were typical of them. 'Helping Mother' no doubt was meant for us females to tackle. 'A Trip To London' probably did not get many takers for although we were only some seventeen miles from the capital, and could see the Crystal Palace winking in the sunshine against the smoky background of the city, there were still a number of children at Chelsfield who had never been to London or, for that matter, on a train to anywhere.

I quite enjoyed writing essays, and had no difficulty in spelling, probably because I came early to reading. But the boys made heavy weather of literary composition, and were forever breaking the silence by asking how to spell 'yesterday' or 'strawberries' or 'carpenter', the sort of words which, I felt impatiently, they could easily have worked out for themselves phonetically.

Mr Clarke used to take our efforts home, and return our books the next day, suitably marked in red ink. Occasionally, he read aloud from one of them, and if it happened to be mine, I was acutely embarrassed. I still think that it is a terrible ordeal to hear or see one's own work in public. Mr Clarke's kind comments on my skill made me cringe. Much easier to bear were the subsequent teasings from the boys about my prowess.

This teasing was kindly. It had nearly killed them to write half a page on the subject set. That one younger than themselves could scribble two or three pages, struck them as peculiar to the point of being idiotic, and they were suitably indulgent.

As time went on, my initial alarm at having to share a classroom with boys gradually faded, and although my closest friends were girls, I began to look more tolerantly at the opposite sex.

I admired their physical strength. They were far better at digging, at trimming hedges, at lifting heavy things and particularly at climbing than we were.

The massive elm trees, which lined the road near St Martin's church, housed a noisy colony of rooks, and I watched one of the boys climb to the top of one of the

trees to collect a rook's egg. It makes me shudder now to remember the incident.

He descended neatly, the egg in his mouth for safety, and seemed absolutely unmoved by his feat. My own pride in being able to climb our small and accommodating yew tree paled into nothing beside this nonchalant exhibition.

On the whole, they were a hardy and agile set and would have been more agile still, I suspect, but for their clothing. Most of them wore thick jackets, some too tight and restricting, and the usual thick leather laced-up boots, often with iron-studded soles, meant that they were handicapped when it came to running and jumping.

We fared better as girls, in lighter clothing and sandals in the summer, although laced-up boots were certainly worn by some in the winter. Wellingtons, for general winter wear, did not come until later.

Our diet, by today's standards, would be considered too starchy, and viewing the contents of those lunches carried by my schoolfellows, this was certainly the case. I was lucky to go home to a well-cooked midday meal.

As well as the ubiquitous eggs at home, we now had plenty of goats' milk, for four goats had been added to the chickens, ducks, and rabbits already kept.

There was no shortage of fruit in the village generally, for beside the usual seasonal garden fruit, starting with rhubarb and gooseberries, and continuing throughout the summer months to the last late plums, the fields yielded splendid strawberries, and after the lorries had carted most of the crop up to Covent Garden, the farmers allowed the villagers to glean what was left.

We probably ate more than we collected for jam-making, but there were always plenty of jewel-bright jars put aside for the winter, and to be given to our poor town-bound relations when they visited.

On one or two occasions I was lucky enough to have my lunch at Groom's the baker's. My mother made the arrangement. For some reason she would not be at home, and I was excited at the thought of sitting in solitary state at one of Groom's marble-topped tables in front of the counter.

No one else ever seemed to have a meal there, although I believe cyclists sometimes came in to re-fresh themselves with tea and buns in the afternoon.

My lunch cost sixpence, and was always the same. I had a boiled egg, bread and butter, and a glass of milk. After that I could choose one of Groom's three cakes, a currant bun, a doughnut or a fairy cake in a frilled paper case. Plenty of starch there, but no doubt I had an apple from home as well.

I could here sounds from the room beyond the shop, and sometimes a shadow was thrown on to the lace curtain which screened the glass door from prying eyes. Probably the eyes on that side were looking to see how I was getting on.

There was a large poster for Mazawattee tea which intrigued me. It showed an Edwardian lady in a velvet coat to the ground and an enormous hat, reclining on a green seat, like those I remembered in London parks.

She was dangling a little box from a gloved hand. Naturally it contained Mazawattee tea, and it was interesting to note that she had no other shopping. Why had she bothered to go to the shops just for that one item? And why had she collapsed on to the bench when even a lady as high-born as she obviously was, could reasonably have been expected to carry such a tiny parcel without undue strain? Or could she be taking it as a present to a distant friend, and was having a rest half-way? Perhaps she had suddenly decided that she could not part with such a treasure after all, and was sitting there before returning home with her parcel? I should like to have enquired of the girl who brought my lunch, and who took my sixpence once I had untied it from the corner of my handkerchief, but I was too shy.

I remembered, however, to thank her politely for looking after me, for my mother had pointed out that Groom's did not usually serve lunches, and we were much obliged to Mr Groom for making an exception in my case.

I suppose that lovely lady with her packet of tea ended on a bonfire one day.

What a pity!

Pageants and People

ONE of those summers in the early twenties brought a memorable occasion.

The West Kent Women's Institute proposed to stage a mammoth pageant showing the history of the area, and it was to take place in the magnificent setting of Lullingstone Castle, only a few miles from the village.

The project was well thought out. At this distance of time, I could not say exactly how many scenes were envisaged, but something between a dozen or twenty would be my guess.

The first scene was to be about the coming of the Romans, and subsequent scenes showed local incidents in mediaeval times, a visit by Queen Elizabeth, a Civil War episode, some Georgian scenes and so on, up to the 1920s. The idea was to allot a scene either to one specific institute or several who were uniting to act one particular incident. The scenes were to be allotted by drawing names from a hat, so to speak, so that one had to abide by the luck of the draw.

Naturally, when this marvellous event was first

mooted, all the ladies hoped for a scene in which they could dress in silks and satins, lace and ribbons, and wear magnificent wigs. The Stuarts were probably first choice—all those long curly wigs and dashing hats with ostrich feathers on the brim—but one or two still had a Victorian dress handed down from a forbear and it was agreed that little shawls, and even bustles, could be quite fetching.

Imagine the dismay at Chelsfield Women's Institute when it was discovered that they had been picked for Scene One, The Coming of the Romans. All thoughts of ostrich feathers, ringlets, or even plaits with pearls interwoven and wimples, had to be abandoned. Luckier institutes would swan about in this splendour, while the Chelsfield contingent would have to be content with clean sacks and old furs hacked into some rough semblance of Ancient Britons' clothing.

Unless, of course, they were Romans. The best-looking would undoubtedly be selected to form a Roman cohort, attired in gold-painted cardboard uniform and sandals, and whoever in charge at Chelsfield had to decide who should be an Ancient Briton and who should be an elegant Roman soldier, had a pretty sticky bit of diplomacy before them.

After the first disappointment, the local ladies set to with a will, sharing bits of old fur coats, getting excited about lengths of sacking, if they were Ancient Britons, and studying diagrams of Roman military costume—cardboard, gold paint and shears at the ready—if they were comely enough to have been chosen for the Roman cohort.

Children were needed, of course, as part of the tribe, and Norah and I were delighted to be dressed in the regulation sacks and furs, and to take part with our mothers.

Rehearsals were held in the garden of a lovely old house not far from the school, called Lilleys. I believe it was burnt down some years later. There, on hot afternoons, our mothers and other Britons limped about barefoot, dodging the pebbles on the gravel, and trying to look suitably engrossed in stirring imaginary pots, skinning imaginary rabbits, rocking imaginary babies, and occasionally rebuking their all-too-real excited children.

We loved it all, and when the great day arrived we piled into lorries supplied by Norah's father and made our way over the hill to Lullingstone Park, laden with

various stuffed animals, an awkward pole with SPQR waving at the top for the Romans, pots, pans, large dolls for British babies and, of course, our picnic lunches.

We all agreed that it was a good thing to be on first, for after that we could sit back and enjoy the show. I remember how united we all felt, a real band of sisters, out to do our best, and to show the rest of West Kent that Chelsfield was a force to be reckoned with.

To be honest, I really don't remember much about the rest of the performance except that the splendid figure of Queen Elizabeth, played by Lady Hart-Dyke, if I remember rightly, on a fine grey horse,

against the setting of Lullingstone Castle and acres of Kentish greenery, has remained with me to this day.

I remembered this pageant when I wrote *Village Diary* years later. Mrs Pringle was then cast as an influential Ancient Briton, but I don't imagine that she enjoyed herself as rapturously as we did over sixty years ago.

The feeling of being part of a community, which had been so strong during the preparations for the pageant, was something which those born in the village naturally took for granted. As newcomers from London, it struck us all as something rare and valuable.

People's talents were known and respected. If a concert or fête were being organised then those in charge knew exactly where to look for support.

The former headmaster's daughter could be counted on for a display of dancing in the Isadora Duncan manner. Another girl was good at lettering and would undertake to do the posters. The Glee Club, to which my father and mother belonged, would render as required. Someone would be game to recite monologues, which would need to be carefully vetted if the rector was to be present.

The cake stall would groan under fruit cakes from Mrs This, shortbread from Mrs That, and Victoria sandwiches from my mother, who always had plenty of eggs.

What is more, these skills were employed willingly. Part of the fun of a village affair was the work that you put into it, and what each person could contribute was soon summed up.

My sister Lil, young as she was, was soon prevailed upon to play the church organ on the odd occasion when the usual organist was absent. I had a more lowly rôle as organ blower, when she was at the keyboard, and pumped a handle up and down in the vestry, one eye on a small weight which travelled between two pencil marks on the wooden screen. If it rose too high then the air ran out, and bedlam ensued. I learnt to dread Lil's pulling out of a stop marked TREMOLO, for then my little weight fairly galloped to the top mark in a series of bounds.

This knowledge of each other's talents extended to their clothes, their eccentricities, their homes and gardens. Neighbours were important, and could prove a blessing or a bane, according to temperament. As children, we frequently ran errands for nearby grown-ups.

On one occasion, our friend Peggy who shared our yew tree, was dispatched by an elderly neighbour of hers to the local ironmonger at Pratts Bottom. She was to order: 'An inexpensive enamel slop bowl', and it was to be delivered promptly.

This somewhat imperious old lady was the wife of a retired clergyman, and everything had to be done with the greatest rectitude.

We accompanied Peggy on her errand, wondering vaguely among ourselves exactly what 'an inexpensive enamel slop bowl' was, and what was its purpose.

Peggy thought it was for washing up. One of us hazarded a guess that it was some sort of basin for tea leaves, although why it should be made of *enamel* when presumably the rest of the tea set would be of *china*, we could not fathom.

'Well, I shall just repeat what she said,' said Peggy, 'and leave it to the shop man.'

We agreed that this was all that could be done, and duly delivered the message.

Luckily, the proprietor seemed to know what was required, and we retired with relief to pursue our own pleasures.

Later, we heard that an enamel chamber pot, *not even swathed in paper*, had been left on the *front doorstep* of that respectable house, and poor Peggy and her mother endured the full force of their neighbour's indignation. Relations remained strained for some months, and Peggy went on strike and said she would never go shopping for anyone ever again.

She had our sympathy.

One of the most welcome errands I was called upon to undertake was the very occasional delivery of a telegram to a nearby neighbour.

Mrs Smith at the Post Office saw me one lunch time, and asked me to take the yellow envelope to our friends next door to my home.

I felt very proud to be entrusted with this official task, and even more over-whelmed when I was given *sixpence*, evidently the statutory GPO fee, for my labours. Sixpence was a fortune then for a child, and no doubt it was rushed to Mrs Bird's for a pound of demerara sugar and a quarter of desiccated coconut.

Not many people received telegrams in those days, and far too few needed to be delivered by me, but what bliss when that occasion came my way!

The people I saw most of, naturally, were my school-fellows. As those three happy years slid by, I grew to view them with affection and admiration.

In many ways, they were older and wiser than I was. Most of the girls had younger brothers or sisters to look after, or seemed to do more for their parents than I was called upon to do. They were knowledge-able about such mysteries as the source of babies, in which I was not particularly interested as I had too many other enthralling things to do.

They noticed clothes, hair styles, and other people's possessions. The boys were not so much objects of attraction, as positive nuisances, demanding attention, being noisy, rough, and sometimes downright vulgar. The girls had a well-developed sense of propriety, and were often shocked at things which I sometimes thought merely amusing.

The school building became as familiar to me as my own home. I grew fond of the grooves in my desk lid, the knots on the floor boards, the reflection of the high windows in the dark background of the portraits of our King and Queen.

I liked the green metal contraptions high on the wall, which had a little metal fist, holding a short rod, on the outside. The boys used to lob their apple cores into them, and it was years later that I was told that these mysterious fixtures were ventilators. Heaven alone knows what sort of insanitary mess was inside!

I liked to hear the droning of the children next door, beyond the pitch-pine partition, as they chanted their tables or learnt a poem. I liked to feel the warmth from the coal fire, and to watch one of the big boys shovelling on the fuel when needed.

I appreciated Mr Clarke's witticisms, his tolerance, and his handling of the top standard boys who could have been obstreperous, so close were they to escape into a larger world.

In fact, the place fitted me as snugly as a cocoon, and lapped in warmth, security and friendship, I thrived as never before.

*

As the dreaded scholarship examination drew nearer, I began to realise just how keenly I should miss my present surroundings.

I had visited my sister's school in Bromley now and again, when there had been an Open Day or Sports Day, and of course had heard all about it from her.

It was here that a few of us from Chelsfield School sat the examination one Saturday morning in spring.

My heart sank at the sight of those long stony corridors, the vast hall, the plethora of classrooms, and the expanse of playing fields.

Everything was beautifully kept. The paintwork inside was glossy and white, a rare thing to find in a school. The parquet floors shone like satin. The glass in the doors and windows gleamed with cleanliness.

There were neat flower beds set among mown lawns, and I longed for something smaller, shabbier and familiar.

In the year before, Margaret from the Post Office had become a successful pupil here, and Mr Clarke had told us in assembly how proud we should all feel.

My heart had gone out to poor Margaret, compelled to stand alone before the school, enduring Mr Clarke's eulogy and—final horror—the clapping of her school-fellows. But she was an equable child, and bore it all very well.

The result of my own effort was not due until June, and I sensed that my parents were anxious. I hoped that I should not disappoint them, but I could hardly bear to think of leaving the village school.

On 17 June 1924, my parents received a letter to say that I had passed. The postman came about eight o'clock, and I was in the garden feeding my rabbits, before setting off for school.

I can see their faces now, full of loving pride, as they held up the letter and called the news to me.

My sandals were wet with dew, my fingers sticky with bran mash, but I hope that I raised a smile to match their own.

Two terrible clouds hovered over me. I should be going to a school just like my first one. It would be big, noisy and competitive. Examinations would loom larger every year. I should have endless possessions, three pairs of shoes, a satchel, a hateful uniform with a panama hat in summer and a black felt in winter. I should be bound round with rules, pestered by prefects, goaded by ambitious school mistresses, harried to death.

The second fear was more immediate. I should have to face the same horrors as Margaret. Would Mr Clarke take pity on me, and let me off the public praise? Could I beg him not to let the children clap? Could I pretend to be ill and stay at home, preferably in the bathroom?

My mother wrote a note to Mr Clarke in case he had not yet heard the amazing news, and it was put into my pocket. She kissed me fondly as I set off. My father, wreathed in smiles, had already departed to Chelsfield station.

I made my way along the lane with my heavy burden. I walked past the violet beds, the walnut trees, the geese splashing in the pond, the shabby shed which housed the shabbier fire-fighting barrow, and came within sight of the school.

Vociferous and excited, my companions rushed about behind the railing, beneath the fluttering lime trees, their hair bobbing in the breeze.

I fingered the letter in my pocket, and mounted the school steps slowly.

A shadow had fallen across my sunlit world. It was never to be quite so bright and carefree again.

Epilogue

One winter morning, over half a century later, the telephone rang. One of the editors of a Sunday magazine asked if I would like to visit my old school and write an article describing it now, and when I attended it so many years ago.

Of course, Chelsfield School sprang to my mind as I listened to further details of length, payment, deadline and so on.

Luckily, I had the forethought to ask who else was contributing to this feature. A few eminent names floated down the wire, including Laurie Lee. My heart sank. Of course, he would write about his village school in Gloucestershire, and with all the skill and charm which I so admired.

'Tell me,' I said, 'Mr Lee is writing about his village school, I suppose?'

'Alas no! It's been closed. He proposes to write about a later school which he attended.'

It's an ill wind that blows nobody any good, and I replied buoyantly. 'In that case, I will visit my old village school in Kent, and let you have the result.'

*

I travelled down from Charing Cross by train, passing through the old familiar stations.

I did not go as far as Chelsfield Station, where I had first stood enraptured by early primroses and larks, for Norah met me at Orpington and drove me to her home at Well Hill.

She was now a grandmother, with lots of fluffy white hair, but her smile and her voice were as gentle as when we first met at the age of eight. Now her grandchild was at our village school, and I should see her there the next day on my official visit.

We woke to torrential rain, and were off in good time, following the school bus. When it stopped outside the school, Norah and I waited in the car watching the children mount those well-known steps to the playground above.

On a morning such as this, we should have arrived in our mackintoshes, shoes soaking, hair dripping, and generally bedraggled. Our successors stepped, dry and immaculate, from the shelter of the bus.

I followed them, half-dreading what I should find after fifty years. Surely, anything must be an anticlimax after the fond dreams I had nurtured for so long.

To my delight, the basic structure was the same, and the playground virtually unchanged, although a glass corridor ran along the back of the building where once Mr Clarke's small sons had climbed up on the desks to look into the classroom.

His house, too, had been incorporated into the school, and the sitting-room where he had lent me *David*

Copperfield was transformed into the school kitchen. I felt uncomfortable there, as though I were a trespasser.

I spent the day with those children, and the kind and elegant young headmaster who showed me everything. It was still miraculously my old school—small, domesticated, secure, but wonderfully refined and beautified. Carpets covered the splintered floorboards whose shiny knots had reminded me of buttered brazil nuts. Bright pictures had taken the place of King George V and his wasp-waisted Queen, and the children themselves were clothed in garments which would have been unimaginably chic to us.

Two little girls discussed their ponies, and I remembered the awe with which my battered scooter had been greeted by my fellows in those distant days. School dinner was served, hot, fragrant platefuls of well-cooked, properly balanced nourishment—although I noticed that greens were still left on the rims. A far cry indeed from those lumps of print-grimed bread I remembered.

There was so much to attract the eye, a tank of goldfish, shelves of bright books, enormous paintings being created with outsize brushes. I thought of the little boys who marched from Miss Ellis's class to Mr Clarke's, so long ago, rulers sticking out from their thick socks, as they made their way to a session of Mechanical Drawing. How much luckier their descendants were!

I spent a few minutes, towards the end of the day, alone in the wet playground. From inside, I could hear the hum of school activity. The lime trees were still there, dripping. The cold Kentish air struck the flesh as keenly as it had always done. The grey roof glistened, the iron railings were beaded with bright drops, a pigeon came down to strut through the puddles, and I was eight years old again.